LOWESTOFT
A Pictorial History

The South Pier and Pier Pavilion in the 1890s.

LOWESTOFT
A Pictorial History

Robert Malster

Phillimore

1991

Published by
PHILLIMORE & CO. LTD.
Shopwyke Hall, Chichester, Sussex

ISBN 0 85033 793 3

Printed and bound in Great Britain by
BIDDLES LTD.
Guildford, Surrey

Dedicated to the memory of Ted Frost (1901-1991),
whose enthusiasm for old Lowestoft was infectious

List of Illustrations

Frontispiece: South Pier and Pier Pavilion, 1890s

Preface and Acknowledgements

It is almost 40 years since Hugh Lees and a few others with a liking for local history used to meet for lunch in Bingham's Restaurant in Lowestoft High Street. Each day as we ate our meal, looking out over Maltster's Score to the Beach and the Roads beyond, we would discuss enthusiastically our researches into the town's past, a subject in which few were then at all interested.

My collection of photographs of the town was founded at that same period when someone at Frederick Norton's tobacconist's shop next to the Post Office in London Road North opened a long-shut cupboard and found a hoard of old postcards, some of them already 50 years old. They were brought out and put on sale at a penny each, and I bought one of each; with 240 pence to the pound I could afford to make quite a collection over a number of visits.

On Sunday mornings Jack Rose and I would wander around the remains of the Beach – the term 'Beach Village' was never used by local people then – and in the evenings I would talk of lifeboat history and other things with Jack Mitchley, Eric Porter, Ted Frost, Bill Soloman and others. To all of them, too numerous to list individually, go my thanks for having encouraged and aided my researches over the years.

My thanks go also to David Butcher, who with great generosity made available to me his knowledge of the town's past, gained through a close study of maps and documents while working on a thesis for the University of East Anglia. Without his advice I would have repeated more than one apocryphal story that was once regarded as history.

Within the scope of this book it has proved impossible to tell the full story of Lowestoft and its people, but I hope that my efforts and those of others already mentioned will encourage the townspeople to take a pride in their town. Some day the town's full history will be written, but that is a task I must leave to others.

Photographs have been provided by the following, whom I wish to thank for their help: East Anglian Film Archive, 157, 158; Ted Frost, 150; Jack Mitchley and Port of Lowestoft Research Society, 151-3. All other photographs are from the author's collection.

Introduction

Lowestoft is the chief centre of population in the half-hundred of Lothingland, that north-eastern corner of Suffolk which has more than once been described as an 'island' with the sea on the east, Lake Lothing on the south, the River Waveney on the west and Breydon Water and Yarmouth harbour on the north. It is likely that in Roman times, when sea levels were higher in relation to the land than they are now and a broad estuary existed between the Saxon Shore fort of Gariannonum and the Roman seaport at Caister-by-Yarmouth, it was indeed an island, with an arm of the sea reaching inland towards Beccles.

Though there was a Roman military site at Corton, just to the north of Lowestoft, in the third and fourth centuries, there seems to be no strong evidence of any settlement on the site of Lowestoft until much later. The name Lowestoft is taken to be Hlodver's toft, the homestead of a Scandinavian settler named Hlodver.

Domesday Book records that no fewer than 18 settlements in the eastern part of Suffolk paid dues of herring, the majority of them to Hugh de Montfort, but Lowestoft was not one of these. Lothu Wistoft, as it was called by the clerk who compiled the Conqueror's survey, was Crown demesne, so the fishery was probably part of the royal estate and therefore not included in the assessment. It was linked with a smaller community called Akethorp which has now entirely disappeared, though a section of a boundary bank on its north-western side is still to be seen. Akethorp occupied the area now covered by modern housing north and north-west of St Margaret's church, up to the edge of the Benjamin Britten School playing field, and there is the possibility that St Margaret's stands on the site of the church of Akethorp served by Ailmar the priest, whose name is recorded in Domesday.

There is no mention in the Domesday survey of a church in connection with Lothu Wistoft, but in later years there was certainly a Chapel of the Good Cross on the site now occupied by part of Pryce's shop in Suffolk Road, commemorated long after it fell into disuse by the name of Chapel Lane, which ran westwards from the south end of the town.

There was also a chapel of ease to St Margaret's that was used by the townspeople to save them the long walk to the parish church. Consenting to a continuation of this practice, the Bishop of Norwich in 1570 gave his permission for 'public prayers to be celebrated' in a chapel in the town, 'the parish church at Lowestoft aforesaid not being so conveniently situated for hearing divine service as could be wished (especially in the winter season)'. The chapel apparently built at that time, with a 'town house', was in use for more than 100 years and was replaced in 1698 by a new building often known, like its predecessor, as the Corncross; this served several functions, being a market cross, a chapel and a 'Town Chamber' in which parish business was transacted, the chamber also being fitted up as a schoolroom.

The Corncross survived until 1874, when it was demolished to make way for what one trader in his advertisements referred to as 'The Commissioners' Mansion', an apparent

1. St Margaret's, the parish church of Lowestoft, dates largely from the 1480s, though the tower and the original spire were in existence much earlier. The church was restored by John Louth Clemence in the 1860s.

jibe at the expensive tastes of the Lowestoft Improvement Commissioners of the time. The 'mansion' survives as part of the present Town Hall.

It is difficult to say just when Lowestoft began to serve as a centre for the surrounding countryside and to become a prosperous and thriving town, but there is no doubt that by the 16th century it was just that. Wills made by some of its inhabitants between 1444 and 1550 show that Lowestoft was at that time as prosperous a community as any in Suffolk, with a number of merchants who became involved not only in local agriculture but in maritime affairs as well.

Some of the town's seamen achieved a degree of affluence that no doubt reflects the extent of their activities in the fishing industry. Early in the 16th century John Powle, mariner, left not only 'my salt and my boat with other things that is mine own at the day of this present will-making' on the Denes but also 'my tenement in Lowestoft

2. A drawing of the Corncross of 1698, which survived until 1874 when it gave way to the earlier part of the present Town Hall.

and all the appurtenances above the cliff and beneath ...'. It is clear enough from the wording of his will that John Powle lived in the area of the High Street on top of the cliff, and had his fish-house and net store on the Denes at its foot.

Even at that stage Lowestoft was assuming the shape it was to have until expansion came in the 19th century, with the main street built along the edge of a sandy cliff, formed many centuries earlier when sea levels were higher, and the commercial premises of the fishing boat owners and fish merchants on the broad stretch of flat sand below.

Defending the Town

Such a situation made Lowestoft open to attack from continental neighbours in time of war, and in 1540 two 'bulwarkes' were built and armed to defend the town and the roads; the sheltered anchorage offshore and a third battery followed. These were no more than earthwork fortifications, each armed with three or four guns, and when the Duke of Norfolk inspected them in 1545 he reported that they were 'but of earth as banks made of turves and so far distant from the town, I think it should be no great adventure for a good puissance to land there and burn the said town'. Perhaps it should not surprise us that two years later the churchwardens of Lowestoft sold some of the church plate to mend the guns and to provide ammunition.

When Robert Kett raised his rebellion in 1549 an armed band seized six guns from the Lowestoft batteries and took them off to bombard Yarmouth. If the people of Lowestoft connived in this attack on their old enemy they lived to regret it, for the Yarmouth men captured the guns and later refused to return them.

Little interest was taken by the town authorities in defence measures until the threat of the Spanish Armada caused hurried fortifications to be erected at a cost of £80, with another £32 spent on mounting the guns and providing ammunition. They were subsequently forced by the Crown to spend another £60 on restoring one of the bulwarks; this amount they deducted from their share of equipping a ship, to the annoyance of their partner in this enforced enterprise, Ipswich.

During the Civil War a number of Royalist gentlemen raised the King's standard at Lowestoft, but this revolt of 1643 proved short lived. Colonel Cromwell himself, who happened to be in Norwich at the time, marched on the town with a small force of regular troops and volunteers.

The confrontation was soon over. Some dragoons crept under the chain the Royalists had drawn across the top of High Street and threatened to fire on the gunner who was serving a couple of the town's cannons emplaced to fire up the street. He fled, and the Parliamentary forces broke the chain and entered the town without encountering further resistance. Cromwell is said to have lodged at the *Swan Inn*, at the head of Swan Score, or Mariners Score as it is known today.

3.   A herring lugger and other fishing boats on the beach, with beachmen keeping watch from one of their 'lookouts', from an engraving after James Stark, *c*.1830.

The cannon that Cromwell's men carried off were later returned to the town when a new battery was constructed near Maid's Acre, at the southern end of the town, to counter a threat from Royalist privateers. This gun emplacement later became the site of the town's major fortification on Battery Green. When in 1656 five Dutch warships lay within musket shot of the shore, however, the guns could not be fired as they had no carriages and no ammunition.

During the Second Dutch War the defences did go into action. The alarm was sounded on 5 February 1666, when a Dutch privateer was seen off the town. Major Thomas Wilde and a band of volunteer gunners hurried down to 'the platform on the Denes at the north end of the town', but as they prepared for action the privateer loosed off a salvo that killed the major – a musket shot hit him in the throat.

In that same war the English and Dutch fleets met some 40 miles south-east of Lowestoft and in a battle that ranged across the North Sea the English gained what Samuel Pepys described as a 'great victory, never known in the world'. Though not fought within sight of the town, the engagement of 3 and 4 June 1665 has gone down in history as the Battle of Lowestoft. For the demoralised Dutch it was a disaster, even if in the best tradition of propaganda, as Pepys tells in his diary, 'the Dutch do relate ... that they are the conquerors'. They lost one of their flag officers, Egbert Meeuwsz Kortenaar, in the first pass, and then their commander-in-chief, Jacob van Wassenaer, Lord of Obdam, was killed when his ship the *Eendracht* was destroyed in an explosion that shook many houses and blew open many windows in The Hague. It was the sight of the *Eendracht*'s destruction as much as the drubbing they had received from the Duke of York's ships that caused the Dutch 'to turn their arses and run', as a seaman in one of the ships of Prince Rupert's squadron so tersely put it. Unhappily for the victors they failed to follow up their success, allowing the survivors of the Dutch fleet to escape to the Texel.

The Lighthouses

Admiral Sir Thomas Allin, who had been knighted for his services in the Second Dutch War, was consulted by Pepys, who had just been elected Master of Trinity House, when in 1676 it was proposed that the existing lighthouses at Lowestoft be rebuilt. Two leading lights had been erected in 1609 to guide shipping through the Stanford Channel, and when these were rebuilt in 1628 one of the pair was repositioned near the top of Swan Score to act as the first 'high light'.

The pile of flints in Belle Vue Park, traditionally said to be the base of the first high light, is in fact the base of one of a pair of warning beacons established by the Marquis of Northampton in 1550;

4. The timber low light was made so that it could be moved along the beach to keep in line with the changing channel through the shoals.

the other stood near the junction of Links Road and Corton Road.

Sir Thomas recommended that one of the new lighthouses to be erected in 1676 should be 'on the hill', as proposed by two Elder Brethren who had been sent down earlier to survey the channels off Lowestoft. The flint and brick tower on the cliff top that was built in that year was topped by a hearth in which a coal fire was kept blazing from sunset to sunrise; on the Denes below was the low light, a wooden structure with a lantern lit by candles.

Although the top of the high light was open in its early days, it was decided before very long to glaze the upper part on the seaward side to prevent sparks from the fire being blown on to nearby houses. The risk of fire was a very real one, for the town had already suffered several disastrous conflagrations, including one in March 1645 that began in a fish-house on the Beach, and spread before a north-easterly gale to involve not only other premises along Whapload Road but a whole block of properties in the High Street above.

The coal fire was replaced in 1777 by an oil-burning 'reflecting cylinder' which was modified and developed until in 1796 it was replaced by Argand burners, in which the oil was vaporised, giving greatly increased illumination.

The timber low light, reconstructed from time to time as the structure decayed, was replaced in 1867 by a tubular steel lighthouse designed, like its predecessors, to be moved along the beach so as to be always in line with the ever-changing Stanford Channel. The

5. Some of these houses in High Street, seen here in 1991, were survivors of the fire of 1645 that spread from below the cliff to involve properties in the town above. The doorway of South Flint House at the top of Wilde's Score bears the date 1586.

high light was replaced by a new tower whose oil-burning lantern first blazed out on 16 February 1874.

The low light was discontinued in 1923 and the high light, electrified in 1938, remains today as an automatic unmanned light.

Lowestoft Porcelain

Just at the time English porcelain factories were seeking to rival Chinese producers of ware that was proving extremely popular in Britain, Hewling Luson, a landowner at Gunton, sent some of the clay found on his estate to an existing factory, probably the Bow factory in London, to find out if it was suitable for the production of porcelain.

Attempts made in 1756 to produce soft-paste porcelain from this clay were unsuccessful; according to Gillingwater the workmen brought in from an existing factory had been bribed to spoil the wares made by Luson. The following year another attempt was made by four Lowestoft men, Robert Brown, a blacksmith, Obed Aldred, ship and fishing boat owner, Philip Walker, gentleman, and John Richman, merchant and boatowner, to set up a factory. In spite of being also 'liable to the same inconveniences as the proprietor of the original undertaking at Gunton' they succeeded in establishing a factory that had a life of more than 40 years, outliving many of its rivals.

The china factory was in Bell Lane, now known as Crown Street, on the site occupied by Winsor & Newton's works, which was formerly a brewery operated by E. & G. Morse. Here a pot kiln was erected in which the ware produced at the factory was fired at a temperature of about 1100°C.

The product of the factory was soft-paste porcelain, made by mixing fusible glass or frit with china clay; at Lowestoft bone-ash was introduced to improve the fire-resistant quality of the china.

The heyday of the china factory coincided with the rise of Lowestoft as a seaside resort, and there is little doubt that many of its products were aimed at the well-to-do visitors who spent the summer in Lowestoft, returning home to Norwich, Ipswich or London only when the autumnal fogs swept in from the North Sea. Some bore the legend 'A Trifle from Lowestoft', while others were inscribed with the names of those for whom they were made to special order.

The factory closed about 1802, probably because the change from wood to coal for firing gave a distinct advantage to the Staffordshire potters, although an apocryphal story blames the downfall of the industry in Lowestoft on the seizure by Napoleon of several thousand pounds'-worth of Lowestoft china when he captured Rotterdam in 1795. It seems unlikely that the Lowestoft factory would have been exporting such an amount of its products to the Continent, where a number of factories were producing their own hard-paste porcelain.

Sea Bathing

One 'Trifle from Lowestoft' is a blue-and-white mug showing a bathing machine on the beach; it is said to have been made in the 1780s. Bathing machines were introduced to Lowestoft in 1769 by the licensee of the *Crown Inn*, Scrivenor Capon, whose advertisement in a local newspaper explained that 'The machine consists of a convenient and Elegant Dressing Room, and of a Bath annexed, which freely admits a Depth of Water not exceeding five feet ... The Bather is perfectly screened from the most inquisitive Eye, by a thick canvas covering to the Bath'. Or, as John Gosling put it in his advertisement for his rival 'commodious Machine' the following year, 'The whole Bath is covered by an Awning from the Eye of Impertinence'.

As well as being the first to introduce bathing machines to the town, Scrivenor Capon was one of the first to realise the need for lodgings in an up-and-coming seaside resort. In the same advertisement in the *Ipswich Journal* in which he acquainted the public of his 'Machine form'd after an Improved model of those at Deal' he declared that he 'hath likewise procured good private lodgings, if they should be preferred to those which he can furnish in his own house; and for the better entertainment of all who shall honour his Bath, will keep a Genteel Ordinary; he always hath the best of Wines and other Liquors, likewise a good Post Chaise with able Horses'.

Each summer the population of the town was swollen by the families of the gentry and successful tradesmen who spent the warmer months by the sea. On 7 and 8 August 1755, the minister and churchwardens went through the parish counting the houses and their inhabitants and found there were 445 houses, all but seven of them occupied; they recorded '2231 Inhabitants and Lodgers' in the Town Book. Virtually all these houses were in High Street and in the lanes running westwards from it, such as Church Lane (St Margaret's Road), Mariners Lane, Bell Lane (Crown Street) and Mill Lane (St Peter's Street).

To the east of High Street were the scores, narrow paths running down the face of the cliff to the area below known as the Beach. The first houses were built in this area during the first decade of the 19th century, and by the end of the century there was a lively community of fishermen and other seafarers living on the Beach. Today it is commonly

6.   The hanging gardens that were eulogised by 19th-century guidebook writers can be seen in this etching, which shows the town from the Denes at the end of the century.

referred to as 'the Beach Village', but right up to the 1950s it was always simply the Beach. The author of the *Lowestoft Guide*, published in 1812, wrote that:

The slope of the hill, upon which the town is built, and which was formerly one continued declivity of barren sand, is now converted by modern improvements, into beautiful hanging gardens, reaching, by a gradual descent, from the dwelling-houses above to the bottom of the hill, and extending nearly from one end of the town to the other.

These gardens are most of them richly planted with various kinds of trees, intermingled with shrubs; and the white alcoves, summer-houses, rustic seats &c., with which they are interspersed, agreeably diversify the scene, as they peep from the dark foliage which surrounds them, and give to the whole an appearance entirely unique ...

At the bottom of these gardens the fish-houses are erected for the purpose of curing the herrings which are caught on this coast; and are so numerous that, had they been built more compactly, they would have been sufficient to form a small town of themselves. Lowestoft derives many conveniences from the fish-houses being thus detached from all other buildings, not the least of which are the easy conveyance of the herrings from the boats, and the avoiding those offensive smells which arise from the draining and smoking of them.

As the seafaring population grew, houses were built on the Beach and along Whapload Way, a road running at the foot of the cliff. At the first census of 1801 the population was more than 2,332, but at the census of 1811 the Overseers of Lowestoft found the number

7. On the right of this lithograph of a brig signalling for a pilot off Lowestoft about 1860, there is a herring lugger. At left is a two-masted beach yawl, perhaps bringing out the pilot. Just ahead of the brig, which is hove to, is the Stanford lightvessel, and in the distance can be seen Lowestoft harbour and the new buildings of South Lowestoft.

8. The sailing drifter *Shades of Evening*, built in 1877 and owned in the village of Mutford, entering harbour in the 1890s. She appears to be heading for the lighthouse on the South Pier, but the tide setting to the northward will keep her clear of the pier.

of men, women and children had risen to 3,180. Asked to what they attributed the increase, they reported that:

> antecedent to the year 1801, Lowestoft had been increasing though slowly both in its buildings and in its population, which may be attributed partly to the resort of Strangers thither for Sea Bathing and partly from the Turnpike Road from London to Yarmouth passing through it. But the rapid increase of its buildings and population since 1801 is to be attributed to the prosperous state of its Fisheries and particularly of its Herring Fishery, great numbers of Persons having been induced to employ their capitals in that concern ...

Fishing

Lowestoft men took part in the herring fishing from the 15th century, and possibly much earlier. A few fishermen had prospered enough to make wills in favour of their children, and from these wills we learn of the use of 'nets both herring and mackerel, with waroppes and boye barrells and all manner of things' which would be instantly recognised by a fisherman of the 20th century.

In spite of having to work off the beach, Lowestoft fishermen not only carried on the herring and mackerel fisheries but engaged in a long battle both in the courts and at sea with neighbouring Yarmouth, which sought to impose its jurisdiction on the landing of fish at Lowestoft and on nearby beaches. Yarmouth's original ascendancy in local maritime matters is to be found in the Statute of Herrings of 1357, and the argument over whether the corporation of Yarmouth could indeed exercise this control went on for more than three centuries, the decision going first one way, then another, as the mouth of Yarmouth haven moved up and down the coast. In the early 14th century the entrance was between Gunton and Corton, within two miles of Lowestoft Ness.

Notwithstanding such rivalry, Lowestoft's fishermen continued to land herring on Lowestoft's beach. Isaac Gillingwater gives a useful description of the trade as it was carried on in the 18th century:

> The vessels carry from 30 to 50 tons and 9 men and boys upon a average, every vessel is generally equipped at the first fitting out with 90 or 100 nets, which are replaced about the middle of the season, by a fresh set of the same quantity and dimensions ... When the fishing vessel arrives on the fishing ground ... she shoots her nets after sunsett from over the side, which extends near a mile in length, and are carried by the tide 7 or 10 miles, each tide. In two hours after shooting the nets they heave the warp by the capstan, and thus draw the net to the vessel; and if few or no fish are perceived, they wear the net out again and drive two hours longer, the same is repeated till morning, unless they get their quantity of fish sooner, or unless the dog-fish should rise, in which case they draw their nets in as quick as possible, set one mast and sail, and go about a mile or two from this destroyer of nets, by whom £50 or upwards is sometimes lost in one night.
>
> Each vessel is furnished with an apartment called a well, into which the fish are conveyed by a sort of a machine, as soon as they are disengaged from the nets. The bottom of the well is full of holes, through which the blood and water runs, and is pumped overboard.
>
> There are two apartments called wings, one on each side of the well, into which the men throw the herring with scoops; a third throws in the salt, while a fourth and fifth man throws up the herrings to the furtherest part of the wings.
>
> By this means the herrings are preserved until the vessel hath got in 10 or 12 last, when she returns to Lowestoft roads, sends the fish ashore in small boats, from whence they are carted to the fish-house. Here they are salted on the floor, in which state they lie two days; they are then washed in vats of fresh water, put on spits, and dried with many fires of billet wood. If the herrings are intended for exportation, they are kept in this state for four or six weeks, when they are packed in casks of 32 gallons, each cask containing 1,000 herrings.

9. A small trawling smack, the *Samaritan*, leaving Lowestoft under sail in the 1920s. The plume of steam issuing from the starboard side is the exhaust from the steam capstan, a refinement which had replaced the old manual capstans by about 1890.

At one stage the government gave bounties to encourage people to invest in the fishery, but it was economic circumstances rather than government aid that brought about a herring boom in the course of the 19th century. The growth of great industrial towns in the Midlands provided a new market for fish, and the advent of the railways provided the means for getting the fish to those markets.

It was the promise of fast transport to new markets that Samuel Morton Peto made to Lowestoft people in the 1840s when he proposed the building of a railway line to link the town to the existing network, and it was a promise that was soon fulfilled. A herring market with a rail siding alongside was one of the facilities provided by Peto when he began to develop the harbour after acquiring it in 1845.

Herring were caught in walls of netting as they rose to the surface during the night, but there were other fish that lived all their time on the sea floor. To catch them an entirely different type of net, a trawl that was dragged across the seabed, had to be used. This type of fishing was carried on largely by fishermen from Barking on the Thames and by West Countrymen from Brixham and Plymouth until the mid-19th century, and men from these ports were among those who began operating from Lowestoft in the middle years of the century. Others came from the Kent and Sussex ports, particularly from Ramsgate.

Smacks from Barking were using Lowestoft harbour in 1851, and they were followed by others from other fishing ports. Soon fishermen and their families from Kent and elsewhere were settling in Lowestoft, and many a well-established Lowestoft family of today has a memory of forebears arriving in the harbour with their furniture and belongings lashed on the smack's deck.

Local owners and crews were not slow to copy the newcomers who exploited newly-discovered fishing grounds in the southern North Sea. Although generally speaking herring fishermen stuck to their trade and did not work at other kinds of fishing, by 1870 some owners were fitting out their herring luggers for trawling after the conclusion of the autumn herring fishing. The so-called 'converter smacks' exchanged the stumpy mast and loose-footed mainsail employed when drifting, for a loftier mast and a more powerful rig suitable for hauling a heavy beam trawl.

As the fishing industry at Lowestoft boomed, the number of men employed in the boats grew by leaps and bounds. It was estimated in 1861 that 1,520 men and boys were engaged in fishing out of a total population of just over 9,500, and 10 years later almost a quarter of the population, by then some 13,500, was at sea in the luggers and smacks.

Many more were employed ashore either in processing the fish or in trades that in one way or another serviced the fishing industry. Some were beatsters, engaged in repairing the nets that were torn by dogfish or damaged in stormy weather; 'beating' is an old English word meaning to repair or make good. Others worked in the fish-houses that in the boom years of the herring industry expanded from their old situation beneath the cliff into the town above.

10. Gowing's ropewalk can be seen stretching across the Denes in this engraving by Rock & Company, dated 1872. In the foreground, nets are being spread to dry after tanning, and at the foot of the cliff are the net stores and smokehouses along Whapload Road.

In these smokehouses the herring were turned into bloaters, kippers and red herring, the latter going mainly for export to overseas markets. Work here was hard and by no means well paid. For a working day that lasted from six in the morning until six o'clock in the afternoon a youngster might in the 1930s have received 25 shillings a week; that was for six days' work. The hanger and striker, whose duties included firing as well as setting the speets and baulks of herring in the smokehouse, was paid £2 5s. a week, this wage reflecting the responsibility resting on his shoulders. If he stirred the fire too much or opened the ventilators so wide that the oak shavings burst into flames instead of merely smouldering, he might cook the herrings instead of curing them.

By the beginning of this century large numbers of boats from Scottish ports were joining in the East Anglian autumn herring fishing, and with them came a great army of workers who arrived in special trains from both the east and west coasts of Scotland. Besides the lassies who gutted the herring landed by the drifters there were many others, who laboured out of sight in the fish-houses or made up the barrels in which the herring were packed for export.

Traders who provided clothing both for the fishermen and for the shore workers prospered while the herring industry expanded. Daniel Lark, who claimed that his business had been established as far back as 1803, advertised himself in 1912 as 'maker of the celebrated Scotch Duffles, Trousers and Sea Boots' and 'Renowned Fisherman's Oil-Clothing of every description'.

Sailmakers were required to provide the sails both for the fishing craft working from Lowestoft and for other vessels using the harbour, and in the days of sail they were always busy, particularly after a 'blow'. Then there were the shipchandlers, the mast and block makers and all the other tradesmen supplying the thriving fleets of luggers and smacks.

Those fleets demanded a continual supply of rope and twine both for their rigging and for the fishing gear they used, keeping many ropemakers and twinespinners in constant employment. A 'patent ropery' was established by the Gowing family in 1790, and by 1844 there were no fewer than 17 twinespinners and ropemakers in the town. The Gowings' ropewalk, a quarter of a mile long, spread across the Denes roughly parallel to Whapload Road. The ropery buildings, which consisted of a winding room, dressing chambers, tar houses, rope store and offices, stood at the southern end of the walk, which remained in the ownership of the Gowing family for more than a century.

Four generations of Gowings were involved in the business, which eventually gave way before the importation of materials produced at Gourock, Bridport and elsewhere. When George Sead Gowing died in 1872, more than 50 fish salesmen and fish buyers preceded the hearse through heavy rain on its way to the funeral service.

19th-Century Improvements

After many centuries as a fishing port, Lowestoft was given a harbour in the 1830s by an ambitious scheme promoted largely by Norwich merchants, who saw the making of a way to the sea at Lowestoft as a means of overcoming the opposition of Yarmouth to their proposals to make 'Norwich a Port'. The first spadeful of earth was dug by Mr. Crisp Brown, a Norwich maltster and merchant, at Lowestoft on 4 September 1827, and shipping was using the harbour by 1831.

The intention of the promoters was not so much to secure the future of the town of Lowestoft as to make a navigation by way of Oulton Broad, the River Waveney, a New Cut across the marshes from Haddiscoe to Reedham, and the River Yare by which sea-

11. Scottish fishworkers carrying baskets or maunds of herring to be packed into barrels for export, seen in a photograph taken in 1909.

The Norwich and Lowestoft
NAVIGATION.
TO BE SOLD,

At the Auction Mart, London, on Wednesday, October 21 (unless previously disposed of by Private Contract, by order of the Commissioners for the Issue of Exchequer Bills in Aid of Public Works, appointed by the Act of 1st and 2nd of William IV. chap. 24, and the Acts therein referred to, and the Acts subsequently passed for amending the same, and authorizing a further issue of Exchequer Bills,

THE NORWICH and LOWESTOFT NAVIGATION, and all Works and Property belonging thereto, and all Rates, Tolls, and Receipts to arise therefrom and made payable to the Company of Proprietors of the Norwich and Lowestoft Navigation, by the Act of 7 and 8 George IV. chap. 42, together with the corporate rights of the said Company under the said Act, and a subsequent Act to amend the same. This public work in its present state opens a communication from Norwich to the Sea, at Lowestoft, by which Sea-borne Vessels, without breaking bulk, are enabled to navigate to Norwich and Beccles, instead of discharging their cargoes into small craft; as heretofore, at Yarmouth. The receipts for tonnage on this Navigation have progressively increased as follow :—

To 10th of August, 1832, £743. 9s. 7d.
    To ditto, 1833, ... £1371. 16s.
    To ditto, 1834,.......... £2007. 17s. 5d.
    To ditto, 1835, ... £2246. 9s. 5d.

For further particulars apply to Winstanley and Sons, Paternoster-row, London, or to Mr. John Winter, Solicitor to the above Commissioners. N. B.—All communications requiring particulars, per post, are requested o be directed, under cover, to the Commissioners for the Issue of Exchequer Bills, South Sea House, London.

12. An advertisement from the *Norwich Mercury* for the sale of the Norwich and Lowestoft Navigation. It is perhaps not entirely without humour that inquiries were directed to the Commissioners for the Issue of Exchequer Bills at South Sea House, London; there were no takers.

going vessels could sail up to the city of Norwich. In spite of the delaying tactics employed by both customs officers and harbour officials at Yarmouth, the first ships to make use of the new route reached Norwich in September 1833.

The opening of the harbour gave a boost to the development of the town, which in 1831 had a population of no more than 4,238. Soon new houses were being built on what had been open land or the gardens of large houses, and in 1832 the Rev. Francis Cunningham, a most popular vicar, laid the first stone of St Peter's, which was to serve for more than a century as a chapel-of-ease to St Margaret's. The architect of St Peter's was John Brown, a nephew of Mr. Crisp Brown, who had inaugurated work on the Norwich and Lowestoft Navigation in 1827.

Sadly the navigation did not live up to the expectations of its promoters. Its income was insufficient to repay the large sums it had borrowed from the Public Works Loan Commissioners for the construction of the harbour and other necessary works. In due course the Norwich and Lowestoft Navigation was put up for sale, but there were no buyers and the Loan Commissioners were left with an unwanted harbour and waterway on their hands. Little was done to keep the harbour in repair, and decay soon set in.

In 1843 six Lowestoft men purchased the harbour for less than £5,000 and set to work to counter the silting of the harbour mouth that had all but ruined the original scheme. Within little more than a year they sold it to Samuel Morton Peto, a builder and railway contractor who had settled in the district while involved in the construction of the Eastern Counties Railway from London to Norwich by way of Cambridge.

Peto earned for himself the title 'father of modern Lowestoft', for he not only reconstructed the harbour, adding an outer harbour to seaward of the original harbour entrance, but built a railway from Reedham to Lowestoft and set about the development of a new town south of the bridge.

13. The awning that protected users of the bathing machines 'from the Eye of Impertinence' can be seen in this Rock print of Battery Green and the Bath Rooms in 1850. Battery Green took its name from Lowestoft's main fortification.

14. The timber structure of Lowestoft Central station, built by Lucas Brothers in 1855 in place of the original station erected in 1846. It was built of first-rate virgin Baltic timber which is still in good condition due to Morton Peto's method of preservation in creosote, a by-product of the coke ovens that provided fuel for the railway engines, which burnt coke rather than coal in the early days.

15. A lively scene on Royal Plain at the entrance to the South Pier, photographed at the turn of the century. Horse-drawn waggonettes were as popular as the later charabancs and coaches.

16.   Old Nelson Street looking towards Battery Green about 1910. Until the construction of the harbour and the laying out of London Road in the 19th century, Old Nelson Street was the main route to the south.

His scheme for South Lowestoft comprised five principal blocks of building extending over half a mile of the seafront. At one end there was the *Royal Hotel*, built by Lucas Brothers in 1848-9 for an enterprising hotelier named Samuel Howett, with villas along the Esplanade and terraces of what were described at the time of their building as 'excellent second-rate houses' in Marine Parade. The *Royal Hotel* was demolished in the 1970s and most of the villas have also gone, but the three terraces survive.

The sheer scale of the project is impressive. The Marine Parade frontage measures no less than 900 ft., and Wellington Terrace and Kirkley Cliff 500 ft. each. It has been said that Peto and his architects and builders emulated in their new town what John Nash had done in London's West End, though replacing the Regency stucco with brick.

The railway not only carried away the fish landed by the town's fishing fleet but brought holidaymakers and day-trippers to the blossoming resort. The railway station itself attracted development and new streets were laid out to the north of Rotterdam Road, named not after the Dutch seaport with which Lowestoft at one time traded but from a pair of houses to the south of St Margaret's church.

17. The Town Hall was built for the Improvement Commissioners in 1857 between Compass Lane and Mariners Lane on the site of the old Corncross. Both the *Star of Hope* on the corner of what had then become known as Compass Street and the *Red Lion* were demolished in 1898, when the Town Hall was rebuilt and extended to provide better offices for the borough council. They are seen here some years before their demise.

For a time there remained a gap between the bottom of High Street and the development around the station, known in the 19th century as South End. This gap was occupied by the grounds of a large house named The Grove, lying between London Road (otherwise known as The Turnpike) and Battery Green, site of the largest of the Lowestoft fortifications. When this estate was sold in 1885 the gap was filled by new shops and streets of substantial town houses, one street taking the name of Grove Road.

Town Government
Lowestoft took its first step up the local government ladder when in 1854 the Lowestoft Improvement Act was obtained uniting Lowestoft and its new suburbs, including Kirkley, into a single administrative entity. Morton Peto was one of the first commissioners, elected by open ballot.

The commissioners were empowered to raise a rate of up to 2s. 6d. in the pound, a restriction which imposed on them the necessity of cutting their cloth to suit their purse. That was doubtless one reason why in 1883 the churchwardens of Lowestoft and Kirkley,

18. One of the Corporation's single-deck trams makes its way northwards past the Town Hall, rebuilt in 1899-1900. During the rebuilding the front of the premises was moved back to widen the road. The photograph was taken about 1910.

who through the Vestry were much involved in local affairs, were asked to call a public meeting to consider steps to obtain a charter giving the town the status of a borough, with a Mayor and Corporation. Such a charter was granted in 1885.

The settlement that had grown up around Mutford Bridge, where the Norwich and Lowestoft Navigation Company had built a lock linking Lake Lothing with Oulton Broad, became in 1904 an urban district under the name of Oulton Broad, and in the 1920s this was incorporated into the borough. The parish of Gunton and most of Pakefield were added in 1934, bringing the total population at that time to over 46,000.

Sadly, Lowestoft lost borough status with local government reorganisation in 1974, when Waveney District came into being and absorbed not only Lowestoft but also Southwold, Beccles, Bungay and Halesworth, and the rural areas around them. The town did, however, remain firmly in Suffolk when some of the northern parishes of Lothingland were transferred to Norfolk.

Progress has not been kind to Lowestoft. The community that had grown up on the Beach has given way to an industrial estate, a new road to carry through traffic has been driven through the heart of the town's residential area, and the decline of the fishing industry has had a pronounced effect on the job prospects of the population.

Yet there are signs that the townspeople are waking up to the need to conserve the best of their heritage of 19th-century buildings, as well as what little remains from earlier centuries. The lead has been given by a handful of dedicated people, including an architect who, in a report, pointed out that if the Peto terraces of South Lowestoft were sympathetically restored 'and their strict discipline were extended into the development of the land in front ... the outcome would rank with some of the grandest architectural set pieces in England'.

The Medieval and Later Town

19.   The sandy cliff and raised beach can be seen in its raw state in this 1890s photograph of Gunton Cliff. The roof and chimneys of the Warren House are visible beyond the ramp leading down to the Denes.

20. Looking down the Ravine at the north end of Lowestoft about 1860. The site of the North Battery is on the right; standing on top of the cliff it did not require the same substantial system of earthworks as the other defences on the lower ground below the cliff.

21. St Margaret's church, seen about 1860 before John Louth Clemence began his restoration. The original building on the site was probably the church of the community named Akethorp and served by Ailmar the priest, as recorded in Domesday Book.

22. A 16th-century flint-walled house in High Street, as it appeared at the beginning of this century. The two blocked windows have since been opened up.

23. High Street at the corner of Compass Street in the 1890s, with the Town Hall that had taken the place of the old Corncross visible beyond the *Star of Hope*.

24. Keystones provide evidence of alterations to these brick-built houses in St Margaret's Plain, seen here at the beginning of this century. The house with the porch was then occupied by Henry Briggs, cabinet-maker and upholsterer.

25. These buildings at the corner of Dukes Head Street and Gun Lane, seen here at the beginning of this century, survived until the area was cleared in the 1970s. The shop with the advertisements for chimney and flue cleaners is that of George Leach, or Leech, gas fitter; the vagueness over spelling is fairly typical of old Lowestoft families.

26. The corner of St Peter's Street and Arnold Street at the beginning of this century. Arnold Street took its name from an old-established local family; Aldous Arnold, merchant, who died in 1792, was described on his memorial in St Margaret's church as 'a man firmly attached to the excellent constitution of his country in church and state'.

27. Two of the town's many public houses can be seen in this turn-of-the-century view of Old Market Plain. Like many other local taverns, the *Old Market Inn* belonged to Youngman, Preston & Company, whose Eagle Brewery stood at the bottom of Rant Score; the stone eagle from the premises survived when a frozen foods firm took them over.

The Scores

28. Linking the High Street and the Beach were a number of narrow alleys known as scores, possibly originating in the gulleys that carried rainwater down the cliff before the town was built. Mariners Score, seen here about 1980 after the building of the Birds Eye Foods factory on the Beach, had a flight of steps and was used only by pedestrians; some were roadways used by wheeled traffic.

29. Looking down Crown Score about 1910. At the foot, on the far side of Whapload Road, are the premises of the Lowestoft Steam Laundry Co. Ltd., and to the left of these can be seen the low light, erected in 1866 to replace earlier timber-framed structures.

30. Looking up Crown Score in the early 1930s, showing one of the street lamps supplied with gas by the Lowestoft Water and Gas Company from their works near the Ness. The gasworks had been established in 1837 by James Malham and was taken over by the water and gas company after its formation in 1852.

31. The High Street entrance to Maltster's Score is seen in this postcard issued at the beginning of the century by William Gwyn, a stationer and printer who had a circulating library at his premises in London Road; he also had a shop in London Road South.

32. Maltster's Score is entered from the High Street through a tunnel beneath the buildings, takes a double turn and runs down the cliff behind what was in the 1950s, when this photograph was taken, Bingham's Restaurant. The crinkle-crankle walls so typical of Suffolk have since gone.

33. Lighthouse Score took its name from the high light, which here seems to be looking down on the row of cottages at the lower end of the score. They were replaced in 1938 by modern council houses. This postcard is postmarked 1913.

The Town Below the Cliff

34. The Beach was the home of many of the town's seafaring men, and also their workplace. These sheds were net stores used by longshore fishermen; they were swept away when the area was redeveloped in the 1960s.

35. Herring nets hang out to dry after tanning in this view of a group of net stores known as the Shoals on Whapload Road taken in the 1950s. In the background is the high light. In these buildings the nets were not only stored but repaired after being damaged by dogfish bites or heavy weather.

36. Christ church was built on the Denes in 1868 to serve the inhabitants of the fast-growing Beach and was extended later in the century. A separate ecclesiastical parish had been formed in 1866 and the church was opened two years later as a memorial to the Rev. Francis Cunningham, who was vicar of Lowestoft from 1830 to 1860 and rector of Pakefield from 1814 to 1855. In spite of being a non-resident rector for 16 years of his incumbency at Pakefield he was a most popular and respected clergyman.

37.   Buildings in East Street photographed in the 1960s. On the left is the North Beach Bethel, built in 1902 and in its time renowned as the most easterly place of worship in Britain.

38.   The low-lying land east of the cliff has always been subjected to periodic flooding, and householders had flood boards which could be slotted into the doorways to attempt to keep out water. This was the result of an unusually high tide in 1905.

Fishing

39. Sailing drifters, still known to the fishermen as 'luggers' in spite of the adoption of a more modern rig, leaving harbour in the 1890s. The crew of the nearer boat are using sweeps to propel the boat towards the pierheads.

40. As the herring fishery reached its peak, scenes like this on the herring market were not uncommon. One worker is using a wooden shovel, known as a roaring shovel, to mix salt with the herring. The peak year was 1913, when some 350 Lowestoft boats and 420 Scots boats fishing from the port landed nearly 535,000 crans; a cran, 37½ Imperial gallons, weighed 28 stone.

41. Three-masted luggers landing herring on the beach not far from the low light, portrayed by E. Duncan in 1854. On the shore lies a laden net barrow, a stretcher-like device used to carry nets to the net chamber.

42. Counting out herring before the adoption of the cran measure in 1908. Four herring made up a warp, 33 warp a long hundred; 100 long hundreds, 13,200 fish, made up a last.

43. In the great days of the herring fishery before the outbreak of war in 1914 long lines of horses and carts waited to take herring from the market to the fishyards, where they were gutted, or to the railway goods yard for despatch by train.

44. The dandy *Oregon* making for the herring market in the Waveney Dock, excavated in the 1880s to cater for the expanding fishery. Built at Lowestoft in 1884, she was owned at the time the photograph was taken in the 1890s by Charles Breach, member of a family well known in the herring trade.

45. The steam drifter *Prosperity*, built at Oulton Broad in 1906 for local owners, leaving the Waveney Dock on her trials crowded with the families and friends of her owners. The first steam drifter built at Lowestoft was launched by John Chambers in 1897, and within a few years all the local sailing drifters had been replaced by powered vessels.

46. Scots fishing boats, some sail, some steam, lying in the inner harbour during an autumn fishing in the early years of this century. Lying near them is a sailing barge loading from a railway truck.

47.   Landing herring on the market in the 1920s. The baskets of herring were swung ashore by the drifter's own tackle, using a small winch set on top of the steam capstan.

48.   On busy days during the autumn fishing every available length of quay was occupied by drifters, berthed with bows on to the quay. This picture shows a scene in the 1920s.

49. Large numbers of barrels were needed to pack the herring which were pickled in brine for export. In preparation for the season coopers made up hundreds of barrels that were stacked on the Denes to await use.

50. A cooper puts the heads on barrels of herring for export to Germany or Russia, while the carter waits to take another load to the steamer lying in the inner harbour that will carry them to the Baltic.

51. Stacks of barrels awaiting filling spread across the Denes at the beginning of the autumn or, as the Lowestoft men termed it, the Home Fishing. Some are already being packed.

52. A beatster repairing nets in the beating chamber of a net store on Whapload Road, in the 1950s. In the days when drifters were numbered by the hundred many beatsters worked at home in addition to those employed in the net store.

53. The chimney of the tan copper is emitting thick smoke as the nets are tanned in a hot solution of cutch, a material derived from oak bark. In the foreground already-tanned nets are hung on the rails to dry, a sight that has disappeared now that the herring fishing is a thing of the past.

54. Below the beating chamber the ransacker sets up the nets, tying the norsels to the netrope. In the old days the ransacker looked over the nets to assess the amount of work to be done; ransack is an old work for search or look over. This photograph, nos. 53, 55 and 56 were all taken in the 1950s.

55. Lowering nets into the tan copper. The nets had to be steeped in the hot cutch solution each time they were brought ashore so as to preserve them; without such treatment the cotton lint would soon rot.

56. Drift nets are hung out to dry on the rails after being tanned. Most of the rails have now disappeared, but many of the posts remain.

57.   The eight-man crew of the steam drifter *Pevensey Castle*, which was fishing for mackerel when this photograph was taken about 1930. Even as recently as 1963 four Lowestoft drifters took part in the mackerel fishing from Newlyn.

58. Shooting the nets on the Smith's Knoll grounds during the autumn fishing of 1953. By 1970 there were no Lowestoft-owned drifters working from the port.

59. The crew packing the last of the fish aboard a Lowestoft trawling smack. The steam capstan used for hauling in the trawl warp stands amidships, and the beam trawl can be seen laid along the port rail.

60. The ketch-rigged smack *Breadwinner*, built at Lowestoft in 1897, in the Trawl Basin.

61. The steam drifter-trawler *Acorn* c.1960 in dock, with an eel fisherman working from a small boat alongside. The curious eel net is thought to have been introduced to Lowestoft by Belgian refugees, who found shelter in the port during the First World War.

62.   The fisheries research vessel *George Bligh* coming through the swing bridge about 1930. Built at Selby in 1917 as a naval trawler, the *George Bligh* was owned by the Ministry of Agriculture and Fisheries, whose research laboratories occupied what had been the *Grand Hotel* at Pakefield.

63.   A busy scene early in the morning on the fish market, with fish landed by the motor trawler being auctioned in the background. The canopy of this section of the market had been rebuilt in concrete by the time this photograph was taken, about 1970.

The Navy

64. Lowestoft was for very many years a base for the fishery protection vessels operated by the Royal Navy to police the North Sea fishing grounds. In the early years of this century the 'flagship' of the fishery protection flotilla was HMS *Hearty*, a smart yacht-like vessel bought for the Navy's surveying service while being built as a tug at Dundee in 1885. Here she is passing through the bridge about 1905.

65. The coastguard vessel *Squirrel* at Lowestoft about 1908. She was replaced on the North Sea fishery patrols in 1911 by the *Watchful*, a larger coastguard vessel built in that year at Aberdeen, and she then moved to Falmouth. Both *Squirrel* and *Watchful* became traditional names for fishery patrol vessels and were given in the 1960s to inshore minesweepers employed on fisheries duties.

66. The torpedo-gunboats *Leda* and *Halcyon* dressed overall for a Lowestoft Regatta just before the First World War. Unsuccessful in their original role of defence against fast torpedo boats, these vessels were employed in the fishery protection service until the outbreak of war.

67. The launching of the second class cruiser HMS *Lowestoft* at Chatham Dockyard on St George's Day, 1913. The seventh naval vessel to bear the town's name, she served throughout the First World War and was broken up in 1931 at Milford Haven.

68. HMS *Leda* moored in the inner harbour before the First World War. Her tall topmasts carry early radio aerials.

69. The third class cruiser HMS *Barham* in Lowestoft harbour in 1905. Built in 1889, she was sold for breaking up just before the outbreak of war in 1914.

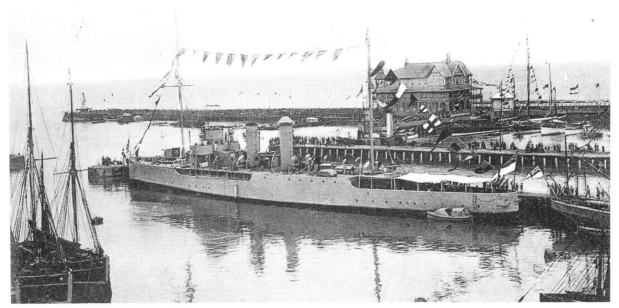

70.   Between the wars Flower-class sloops such as the *Godetia* were employed on fishery protection duties, and were a familiar sight in Lowestoft harbour. The *Godetia* put to sea one night in April 1925 to assist the airship R.33 which had broken away from the mooring mast at Pulham in Norfolk and had been blown out over the North Sea. The *Godetia* was broken up in 1937.

71.   The Algerine-class minesweeper HMS *Mariner* leaving harbour in the 1950s. The green flag on the pierhead is a signal that one of HM ships is leaving and that the harbour is closed to all other vessels for the time being. The *Mariner* was sold to the Burmese navy in 1958.

The Harbour

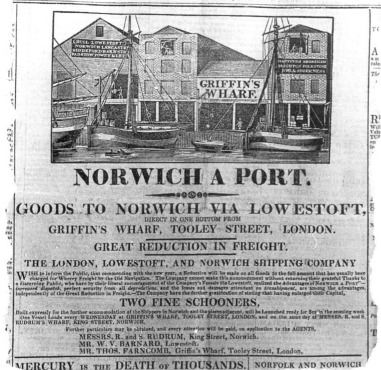

72. Lowestoft harbour was part of the scheme promoted largely by Norwich merchants to make Norwich a Port, a slogan used in this advertisement of 1834 for the London, Lowestoft and Norwich Shipping Company. The block shows the London end of the service at Griffin's Wharf, Tooley Street. Two of the company's vessels, the *City of Norwich* and the *Squire*, were the first ships to reach Norwich by way of Lowestoft harbour and the Haddiscoe New Cut, in September 1833.

73. A brig making for the harbour entrance in the 1830s, before any piers had been extended out into the sea. Beyond the brig is Kirkley Cliff and St Peter's church, Kirkley.

74. The lock at Mutford Bridge, separating the salt water of Lake Lothing from the fresh water of Oulton Broad. This lock was tidal on both sides, making it necessary for four sets of gates to be installed. The engraving is contemporary with the building of the lock in the 1830s.

75. The cattle sheds in the outer harbour, built to accommodate cattle brought from Denmark by the vessels of the North of Europe Steam Navigation Company, an ill-fated enterprise set up by Sir Samuel Morton Peto in the 1850s. The paddle tug *Powerful*, built of wood at Poplar in 1857, was one of the first harbour tugs in the port. This carte-de-visite photograph dates from the 1860s.

76. The lighthouses on the pierheads of the new outer harbour constructed in the 1840s were built of timber, and had an ornate canopy around the base. They are seen here in the 1860s.

77. Morton Peto promised the fishing community that fish landed by the Lowestoft fishing fleet would be delivered fresh in Manchester by railway. This is the fish market that he erected on the north pier in 1856.

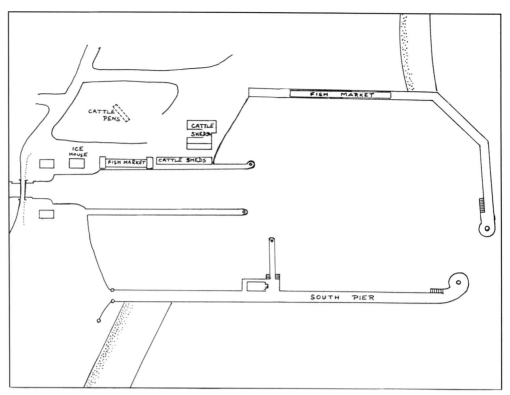

78. A sketch plan of the harbour as it was in 1856 when Peto completed his extension, forming a new outer harbour. The old harbour piers did not project far enough to prevent silting of the entrance.

79. The paddle tugs *Imperial* and *Rainbow*, both belonging to the Great Eastern Railway Company, towing sailing drifters out between the pierheads in the late 1890s. The coming of the tugs gave great assistance to the fishermen, but was resented by the beachmen, professional salvagers.

80. A small trawling smack or tosher, the *Glimpse*, built at Brixham in 1888, entering harbour in the 1890s. The bowsprit has already been run in, preparatory to berthing at the fish market.

81. Two trawling smacks, *Strive* and *Swordfish*, lying in the inner harbour about 1890. In the foreground is the patent slip on which vessels were hauled out for repair, an alternative to taking them into the dry dock further along the quay.

82. The Waveney Dock, officially opened on 1 October 1883, was constructed by the Great Eastern Railway Company to provide accommodation for the growing fishing fleet. The cast-iron brackets supporting the roof timbers of the fish market bear the company's monogram.

83. The only boats alongside the market in this view of the Waveney Dock are shrimpers, which trawled for the shrimps beloved of holidaymakers. When this photograph was taken, *c*.1904, work had already begun on a new dock just to the north, opened in 1906 as the Hamilton Dock.

84. A Russian wooden barquentine, probably laden with timber, is towed up the inner harbour about 1912. On the left a river steamer waits to leave for Beccles with holidaymakers. On the North Quay towards the right is the engineering works built for the North of Europe Steam Navigation Company in the 1850s and the sheerlegs used for installing engines and boilers in ships built at the Lowestoft shipyards.

The Harbour, Lowestoft.

85. On the north side of the bridge was the thatched ice house, used to store ice brought from Norway by sailing ships. Ice was used in great quantities by the fishing industry; the importation of fiord ice became unnecessary when the East Anglian Ice Company was formed in 1898 to manufacture 'artificial' ice in a factory on the south side of the harbour.

86. The harbour tugs *Imperial*, nearest camera, *Despatch* and *Rainbow* in the yacht basin around the turn of the century. Just outside the harbour is one of the fishery protection vessels, still in the black and white paint of the Victorian navy.

87. The barquentine *Alice Sterry* owned by one of the Lowestoft coal merchants, being towed through the swing bridge to her berth in the inner harbour just before the turn of the century. The bridge had been built in the year of Queen Victoria's diamond jubilee to replace the ageing swing bridge, which had been opened in 1830 when the harbour was being constructed.

88. The paddle tug *Rainbow*, built of iron at Cubitt Town on the Thames in 1864, lying in the outer harbour.

The Bridge

89. The original swing bridge of 1830 seen in a picture from Rock's *Royal Cabinet Album of Lowestoft*, published about 1880. It spanned what was originally the sea lock, giving access to the harbour; there were lock gates to pen the water in the harbour, but attacks by teredo worm rendered these inoperative within a few years.

90. The bridge has just closed behind the paddle tug *Powerful* in this photograph of about 1870, which also shows on the right the original fish market which preceded Peto's, seen in Plate 77. A coal wherry is being loaded in the foreground.

91. With the coming of the electric trams in 1903, special arrangements had to be made so that they could run across the swing bridge. The overhead line equipment was fitted with a device that switched off the current both on the bridge and for some distance on either side as soon as the bridge was tilted before being swung.

92. The steam trawler *Valeria*, built of iron at Beverley in Yorkshire in 1898 and owned by Consolidated Fisheries Ltd., passing through the bridge on her way to the ice factory to load ice, just before the Second World War. The *Valeria* was sunk by a bombing attack off the Welsh coast in 1940.

The New Suburbs

93. The Esplanade was part of Sir Morton Peto's development of South Lowestoft, and was relatively new when this photograph was taken in the 1860s. In the background is Wellington Terrace, one of three imposing terraces in which Peto's architect, John Thomas, sought to achieve in brick what John Nash had done in London 30 years earlier using stucco. There is a story that Sir Morton bought the land south of the harbour on which he built his new town for a mere £200, which the Improvement Commissioners considered a handsome offer for what was little more than waste ground.

94.   Peto's new town seen from the fishmarket lookout, with the *Royal Hotel* at left, St John's church and the *Harbour Hotel* towards the right and Pier Terrace at the extreme right. In front of the *Royal Hotel* can be seen the original clubhouse of the Norfolk and Suffolk Yacht Club, formed in 1859; the club gained the 'Royal' prefix in 1898, some years after this photograph was taken. When replaced in 1903, this clubhouse was moved to the Crown Meadow to become a sports pavilion.

95.   The new town, looking northwards from Kirkley Cliff in the 1890s, with the 'excellent second-rate houses' of Marine Parade on the left and the semi-detached houses of the Esplanade in the middle of the picture.

96. The *Royal Hotel*, which in its early days under Mr. Samuel Howett provided such superior service 'that the most fastidious and cynical of travellers would be at a loss for a subject whereon to indulge their spleen', seen from the South Pier in the 1890s.

97. Vehicles waiting to leave Royal Plain for Southwold and other places in the 1890s, with the spire of St John's in the background. Those on the left were owned by Henry Gage, who operated from the *Royal Hotel* stables, seen behind the building on the right; the one on the right belonged to John Newruck, who had premises in Clapham Road. Earlier in the century H. Gage had been based at the *Crown Hotel* yard in High Street (see endpaper).

98. In this print from the 1850s, the name of Howett can be seen on the north wall of the *Royal Hotel*. Samuel Howett came to Lowestoft after a period as proprietor of the *Royal Hotel* in Norwich, one of that city's premier hotels.

99. The grand façade of Wellington Terrace, one of the impressive blocks of buildings that made up Peto's new town south of the bridge, seen in a print of 1858.

100. Some 40 years on, Marine Parade was gaining something of the appearance of a bewhiskered Victorian gentleman as the creepers took over.

101 & 102. St John's church was built by Lucas Brothers in 1853 at the expense of Sir Morton Peto, to serve the new town. The building was designed by John Louth Clemence, who incorporated a hagioscope or 'squint' into the pier of the north transept and chancel arches to enable the congregation there to see the pulpit and reading desk. The photograph of the interior shows the decorations for a harvest of the sea service, held each year to give thanks for the herring fishery; among the decorations are the name pennants of local drifters.

103. St John's church was declared redundant in the 1970s and was demolished.

104. London Road South at the junction with Waterloo Road, c.1904, showing the newly-laid tramlines for the electric trams which first ran on 22 July 1903. The town council had obtained an Act of Parliament in 1901, authorising the construction of tramways within the borough. The gabled building on the right-hand side of the road is the Grand roller-skating rink, later to become a cinema.

105 & 106. St Peter's church, Kirkley, has had a particularly chequered history, for it lay in ruins for many years. What is to be seen of the church today is largely the result of Victorian rebuilding and enlargement at a time when the parish of Kirkley was becoming a suburb of Lowestoft. The iron screen seen in the interior view dates from 1896.

107 & 108.   St Matthew's church was built in 1899 as a mission church in a poor area of Kirkley. The rood screen was brought from St Peter's, the parish church, and re-erected in the new mission church; it had been a memorial to the wife of Edward Kerrison Harvey, who lived in one of the large houses on the Esplanade.

The South Pier

109. Seen here in the 1890s, the South
Pier, part of Peto's reconstruction of the
harbour, became a popular promenade
for the holidaymakers who flocked to
Lowestoft following the building of the
new town south of the bridge. The iron-
framed pier pavilion was opened in 1891
to replace the old reading rooms
destroyed by fire in 1885.

110.   Crowds watching a Punch and Judy show in what became known as Children's Corner, with the pier pavilion in the background, seen in a turn-of-the-century photograph. Mr. Punch has remained a seaside favourite, though there have been changes in his show: Old Nick with his horns has changed into a crocodile and the beadle has turned into a policeman.

111.   The statue of a triton, which was part of Peto's Esplanade layout, can be seen in this view of the South Pier taken from the *Royal Hotel* at the turn of the century. The Great-Eastern Railway poster board at the entrance to the pier serves as a reminder of the role played by the company in developing Lowestoft both as a port and as a seaside resort.

112. The entrance to the South Pier in the 1860s. In the left background is the original reading room where, we are told (in 1866), 'balls are held during the season, which cannot fail to prove a great attraction to the votaries of terpsichore'.

113. The old reading room on the South Pier, destroyed in a spectacular blaze in 1885. Building of the ornate iron-framed pavilion that took its place began three years later; the foundations for the pavilion were somewhat elaborate, as piles had to be driven into the seabed to support the superstructure.

114 & 115.   In Edwardian times the South Pier became a favourite haunt of holidaymakers who sat listening to the band or just enjoying the sunshine. 'In addition to the entertaining music of a first-class military band and vocalists', we are told in an old guidebook, 'the Pier, by virtue of its situation, is in the very heart of a number of diversions, and it is rare indeed for a Pier to have the advantage of being in the main current of the shipping, yachting and fishing life of the place ... another interesting sight afforded by this Pier is the Breakwater, which in rough weather throws up charming mountains of spray. These occasionally also add to the amusement of visitors as they see one and another receive an unexpected shower-bath ...'.

116. The Edwardian seaside. Looking rather overdressed for the beach, a group of youngsters play on a groyne, while one of the Royal Navy's torpedo-gunboats employed on fishery protection duties with black hull, white upperworks and buff funnels lies at anchor in the Roads.

117. The private lifeboat *Carolina Hamilton* was built for lifesaving work after a sad episode in 1882 when the Lowestoft lifeboat, belonging to the Royal National Life-Boat Institution, failed to go to the assistance of a number of vessels wrecked near the harbour. Most of her life was spent as a pleasure trip boat, though. She is here seen approaching the pier steps from which she operated.

118. 'Going for a sail, sir?' The *Carolina Hamilton* can be seen between the steps and the Pier Pavilion in this postcard of *c*.1905.

119. A motor coach has joined the horse-drawn vehicles in this view of Royal Plain, *c*.1913. The yacht club can be seen on the extreme left.

120. The private lifeboat lies at the pier steps as the paddle steamer *Lord Nelson*, belonging to the Great Yarmouth Steam Tug Company, enters the harbour crowded with holidaymakers in Edwardian days.

121. The clubhouse of the Royal Norfolk and Suffolk Yacht Club, designed by Norwich architects G. and F. Skipper, was opened on 11 July 1903 by Lord Claud Hamilton, chairman of the Great Eastern Railway Company, who had paid for the building. The premises were leased from the railway company until 1948, when they were purchased by the club.

122. The entrance to the South Pier in the 1920s. A poster advertises Mark Hambourg, the pianist, appearing at the Sparrow's Nest Theatre.

123. There had been many changes on the Esplanade since Sir Morton Peto laid out his new town 70 years earlier, but in the 1920s the Tritons were a prominent feature of the scene, as they still are today.

The Claremont Pier

124.   The Claremont Pier was constructed in 1903 by the Coast Development Corporation to serve as a stopping place for the Belle steamers which operated a service between London and Yarmouth. The donkeys that provided rides for children had their stand in the pier approach.

125.   One of the Belle steamers lying at the Claremont Pier, c.1910. In the foreground are two bathing machines, successors to those introduced by Scrivenor Capon in 1769.

126. The entrance to the Claremont Pier in the 1920s when dancing on the pier was only one of the attractions that brought holidaymakers to the booking office. Excursion steamers continued to operate from the pier in the 1930s, and the first evacuees from London came to the pier in 1939 in the General Steam Navigation Company's vessels.

127. Like the donkeys, the goat carts that had a stand near the pier proved a great attraction to Edwardian youngsters in their sailor suits.

128.   Looking south from the Claremont Pier, *c*.1920, with the Victoria Bathing Chalets lining the back of the beach and the *Empire Hotel*, built at the turn of the century and converted in the 1920s into St Luke's Hospital for the Metropolitan Asylums Board, on top of the cliff.

Pakefield

129. A group of old cottages at Pakefield *c.*1910, known perhaps appropriately as Flea and Bug Row, and still occupied by fishermen and their families. The cliff edge, which can be seen at the end of the street, advanced inland over the years and many such houses were destroyed as land was lost.

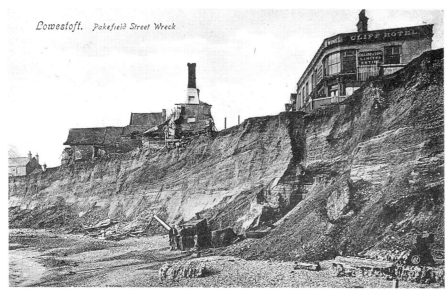

130. A postcard of 1906, showing the destruction caused by the sea's encroachment at Pakefield. Between the turn of the century and the 1930s about ninety houses were lost in the village; the *Cliff Hotel* itself went down the cliff.

131. The new Pakefield. A view of Pakefield Road with South Cliff Congregational church and Edwardian terraces, and youngsters with a donkey cart, just before the First World War.

Oulton Broad

132. The Free Quay at Oulton Broad in the first decade of the century, before the laying out of Nicholas Everitt Park. Oulton Broad, formerly known as Mutford Bridge, became a civil parish only in 1904, being formed out of parts of the parishes of Oulton and Carlton Colville; it later became part of the borough of Lowestoft.

133. The same scene in the 1930s, with Nicholas Everitt Park, given to the borough by Mr. Howard Hollingsworth, in the left background. On the broad is the tank barge *Angloco* which carried petrol from Oulton Broad to Norwich for more than 30 years.

134. St Mark's church at Oulton Broad was built in 1883-4 as a chapel of ease to St Peter's at Carlton Colville, nearly two miles from the growing community around Mutford Bridge. Only in 1931 did it become a parish church in its own right.

135. The opening of St Mark's Institute in Victoria Road, Oulton Broad, on 18 February 1909.

Sparrow's Nest

136. Sparrow's Nest, which takes its name from the Sparrow family of Worlingham, near Beccles, who had a summer residence here, was bought by Lowestoft Corporation in 1897 and laid out as a public park. The bowling green cottage seen here about 1910 is now the Lowestoft and East Suffolk Maritime Society's maritime museum.

137.   Sparrow's Nest House was at one time the home of Baron Alderson. During the Second World War Sparrow's Nest became HMS *Europa*, depot of the Royal Naval Patrol Service, and part of the house now contains a museum dealing with the history of the RNPS, whose memorial stands in Belle Vue Park.

138.   The Sparrow's Nest Theatre was opened in 1913 and was well used both for summer shows and for local events such as dancing displays and Scout Gang Shows for many years. Elsie and Doris Waters were appearing in the summer show here in 1939 when they were evicted from their dressing rooms by naval personnel who were setting up the RNPS depot.

Belle Vue Park and Gunton Cliff

139. Belle Vue Park was laid out in 1874 on an area of heathland known as The Bleach; it had previously been used for laying out washing to bleach in the sun. The park-keeper's thatched house is a fine example of a Victorian *cottage ornée*.

140. Looking north from the lower part of Belle Vue Park in the 1880s. Gunton Cliff is still in its rough state and the building of houses along the crest of the cliff has not yet begun.

141. Belle Vue Park when first
laid out, looking rather bare. Cart
Score runs up between the park
and Sparrow's Nest, and the
Ravine is visible in the foreground.

142. A view at the beginning of
this century from the same
position as Plate 140, with the
first houses appearing on
Gunton Cliff and buildings also
at the bottom of the Ravine.

143. The town begins to
expand northwards: houses
in Lyndhurst Road, between
Corton Road and Gunton
Cliff, built at the beginning
of the century. The picture
was taken about 1910, by
which time the gardens were
maturing.

Trade and Industry

144.   The railway not only brought visitors to the town but also promoted the local trades. In this view of Lowestoft Central station, c.1910, can be seen a Great Eastern Railway omnibus, a Thornycroft, fitted with a charabanc body for the service to Southwold, which was inaugurated in 1904. In the left foreground can be seen the railway crossing the road to reach the docks.

145. On the right of this view of London Road North, *c*.1925, is the Bon Marché, the department store occupied by Tuttle & Sons Ltd., a firm which closed down only in recent years. In the 1890s, when Henry Tuttle & Son had just moved to the Bon Marché to carry on the business of linen drapers, they were also grocers in High Street and Commercial Road. In the middle of the picture are buildings occupying an island site in front of the railway station.

146. The *Suffolk Hotel*, built in the 1870s to replace the earlier inn at which Edward Fitzgerald liked to drink with his fisherman friend Posh Fletcher, and the area in front of the station after the buildings on the island site had been cleared away. Taken in the late 1920s, this photograph shows two United buses, one on the Kessingland Beach service, waiting to depart; one of the Guy buses purchased by Lowestoft Corporation in 1926 is coming down London Road North.

147. An interesting piece of 19th-century advertising: J. Thirtle's rather mixed business in High Street 'opposite the market place', then on land at the corner of Compass Street, had a long history. By the 1870s Thomas Elven Thirtle was an ironmonger at 45 High Street, and by the turn of the century he had expanded his business into no. 47 as well. Later in this century the same premises were occupied by George Nelson Hayes, ironmonger, whose business is still remembered in the town.

J. THIRTLE'S
CHEAP
TEA, GROCERY
AND
IRONMONGERY
WAREHOUSE,

High Street, Lowestoft.

J. T. having engaged commodious Premises, opposite the Market Place, for carrying on the above trades, begs to inform the Public in general that he intends offering Goods connected with the same, for **Ready Money,** at such prices as will ensure him their patronage and support, which he hopes by strict personal attention to merit.

BUILDERS & CARPENTERS
Supplied on Liberal Terms.

CRISP, Printer, Bookseller, Stationer, &c. High-Street, Lowestoft.

148. Ironmongers supplied large quantities of nails, bolts and similar items to the builders of wooden ships who set up their yards beside the harbour; before the opening of the harbour ships and boats were built on the Beach. In the 1920s John Chambers Ltd., at their Oulton Broad yard, built a number of wooden lighters for the Mersey, of which this is one.

149. A sparmaker at work with his drawknife shaping a mast for a drifter in the 1950s. Hand tools such as drawknife and adze continued to be used by craftsmen in the shipbuilding industry until very recently.

150. The sheerlegs on the North Quay is used to hoist the boiler into a steam drifter built at John Chambers' No. 3 yard at Oulton Broad; the engine stands on the quay awaiting installation. The sketch is by Ted Frost, who served his apprenticeship as a shipwright with John Chambers between 1916 and 1921.

151.   A group of workers at John Chambers' No. 3 yard in the 1920s, when steel ships were being built there. The yard lay between Harbour Road at Oulton Broad and Lake Lothing; although the company closed down in 1930 many of the buildings used by Chambers still exist.

152.   A scene in the platers' shop at Chambers' No. 3 yard, a single-storey building of brick, asbestos cladding and glass some 200 ft. long, also in the 1920s. Steel angle is being bent to shape by hand in the foreground.

153. Three steam coasters, the *Melcombe Regis*, *Salcombe Regis* and *Marjorie Mellonie*, at the fitting out quay after launching from Chambers' yard in the early 1920s. One of them, the *Salcombe Regis*, finished up trading on the Argentine coast and up the River Plate.

154. Netmaking was once an important industry in Lowestoft. Here, workers at Beetons' Sunrise Works on the Beach are finishing machine-made nets by hand in the 1940s. Looms for netmaking were developed between 1820 and 1850 as the result of an invention by James Patterson, of Musselburgh.

155. A tie-on label affixed to nets produced at Lowestoft by Beetons Ltd. Such labels were being used up to the 1940s.

Best Quality
Fishing Net

MANUFACTURERS OF NETS AND CORDS
FROM ALL NATURAL AND SYNTHETIC FIBRES

TWINE No...

LENGTH...

MESH..

DEPTH...

BEETONS LTD.
SUNRISE NET WORKS
LOWESTOFT - ENGLAND

East Anglian Ice & Cold Storage Co. Ltd., Lowestoft
MAKERS OF CLEAR TABLE ICE :: DAILY OUTPUT 250 TONS
Above is Photograph of one block 18ft. x 9ft. x 1ft. thick, Weight 3 tons

South Side Inner Harbour, Lowestoft § **Branch:——King Street, Norwich**
Telegrams : "Freezing, Lowestoft" § Telegrams: "Freezing, Norwich"
Phone : Factory 78. Trawl Market 204. § Telephone : Norwich 1115

156. Ice was important to the Lowestoft fishing industry, which used many tons of ice for preserving the catches. This advertisement for the East Anglian Ice & Cold Storage Co. Ltd., established in 1898 by W. F. Cockrell for the manufacture of ice in a factory on the south side of the harbour, dates from the 1920s.

157. A proportion of the fish landed at Lowestoft was canned in factories that are said to have had their origin when James and Archibald Maconochie began pickling onions in the kitchen of their home in Raglan Street. Herring are here being packed into cans in the Co-operative Wholesale Society's factory in Waveney Drive about 1930.

Sport and Leisure

158. The yawl match at the 1853 Lowestoft Regatta, watched by large crowds on the beach and the North and South Piers. The Eastern Counties Railway ran excursion trains to bring visitors to the town for the regatta, which was an event not only for yachtsmen but also for the beachmen, whose yawls competed for prize money totalling £30.

159. Beach yawls, the beachmen's rowing gigs and fishermen's beach punts from Lowestoft, Pakefield and Kessingland all had their races at the 1871 Kirkley and Pakefield Marine Regatta, of which this is the programme.

160.   Lowestoft harbour on regatta day, 1882. A number of smacks, which had their own race in the programme, can be seen on the left. On the extreme right is the reading room on the South Pier, burnt down three years later.

161.   Craft waiting to take part in the regatta, probably in 1896. The *Olga*, the smart-looking wherry on the outside of the group, was new from Hall's yard at Reedham in that year, and was the winner of the wherry race on her first appearance.

162. Water sports, which usually concluded with a 'duck hunt', formed a popular part of the regatta programme. The swimming races took place in the outer harbour alongside the South Pier, which provided a convenient grandstand for these as well as for the yacht racing.

163. Lowestoft's first theatre was a former fish-house in Blue Anchor Lane, today's Dukes Head Street. Later a new theatre was erected for the Fisher Circuit in Bell Lane, now Crown Street, and this theatre survives as the Crown Street Hall, having become Assembly Rooms in the 1830s when the theatrical business was in decline. Further along the street can be seen the former E. & G. Morse brewery, on the site of the porcelain factory which operated in the second half of the 18th century.

164. The Grand roller skating rink in
London Road South, seen here about
1912, had opened as a swimming pool,
and later in its life was converted to a
cinema. Roller skating had become
popular in the town much earlier, an
outdoor rink lined with flowerbeds having
been opened in the Marina in the 1870s.

165. The Hippodrome on Battery Green
Road, seen here c.1980 in its days as a
bingo hall, was built about the turn of the
century by George Gilbert as a circus,
with a roof that could be opened out in
good weather. Next door are the premises
of the Gourock Ropework Co. Ltd., here
occupied by the ironmongery firm of R. J.
Pryce & Co. whose main shop was, and is,
in Suffolk Road.

166. An advertising postcard for *Charley's Aunt* at the Marina Theatre, which took its name from the thoroughfare in which it was built in 1901. Like other places of entertainment in the town, the Marina later became a cinema; today it is the sole survivor of the town's 'picture palaces'.

167. The 1st XI football team of Lowestoft College, 1906-7. The college, whose headmaster was the Rev. John Clegg, occupied premises in Gordon Road in the first decade of this century.

Beachmen and Lifeboats

168.   The Lowestoft lifeboat *Frances Ann*, the world's first sailing lifeboat, putting to sea about 1820. The *Frances Ann* was built for the Suffolk Humane Society by local boatbuilder Batchelor Barcham in 1807 to a design by Lionel Lukin and is credited with having saved more than 300 lives over the course of 40 years. The painting of this incident is among the exhibits in the Lowestoft and East Suffolk Maritime Society's museum at Sparrow's Nest.

169. The lifeboats operated by the Suffolk Humane Society and later by the Royal National Lifeboat Institution were manned by beachmen, professional salvagers who formed themselves into companies to carry on their work. The beach companies, which were early co-operatives, owned a variety of boats, but the principal type was the yawl or yoll, a large clinker-built open pulling and sailing boat. The illustration from the *Illustrated Times* of 20 November 1858 shows a yawl being launched from Lowestoft beach in bad weather; the low light can be seen in the right background.

170. Lowestoft's first lifeboat was a pulling boat built by Henry Greathead at South Shields in 1801 and provided by a fund raised by Robert Sparrow, whose family gave its name to Sparrow's Nest, and the Rev. Francis Bowness, rector of Gunton. Even after a carriage had been built for it, similar to that in the drawing, the beachmen refused to use the boat since they regarded it as unsuitable for bad weather work.

171. One of those who was very active with the *Frances Ann* was Lieutenant, later Commander, Samuel Fielding Harmer. Not only did he serve in this boat under another naval officer, Lieutenant Samuel Thomas Carter, but he proposed certain alterations in 1825 to obtain 'an increase in buoyancy in the lifeboat'. It is thought he might have introduced the principle of water ballast that was a feature of the Norfolk and Suffolk type of lifeboat developed from the *Frances Ann*.

172. Every window along the seafront was occupied by spectators when on 1 November 1859 the lifeboat *Victoria* under Coxswain Bob Hook rescued the crew of the steamer *Shamrock* after it had run on to the Holm Sand. The 14 men of the *Shamrock* had to be hauled one by one through the water to the lifeboat, as shown in this contemporary engraving.

173. The lifeboat shed on the Beach, seen about 1960 after the doors had been removed and the end wall bricked up. No longer required for the lifeboat, which was kept afloat in the harbour, the shed was used by a haulage firm for maintaining its lorries.

174.   The Pakefield lifeboat, *The Two Sisters Mary and Hannah*, with her crew and launchers in the first decade of this century. Built by a Lowestoft boatbuilder in 1872 at a cost of £291, this boat was replaced in 1910 by a new boat costing £1,934; rising costs are nothing new.

Bibliography

Beamish, J., *Lowestoft Reminiscences* (Lowestoft, Flood & Son, 1952).

Boon, J. M., *A Hundred Years of Service, 1853-1953* (Lowestoft Water and Gas Company, 1953).

Butcher, D. R., *The Driftermen* (Reading, Tops'l Books, 1979).

Butcher, D. R., *The Trawlermen* (Reading, Tops'l Books, 1980).

Butcher, D. R., *Living from the Sea* (Reading, Tops'l Books, 1982).

Butcher, D. R., *Following the Fishing* (Newton Abbot, Tops'l Books, 1987).

Butcher, D. R., *The Growth and Development of Pre-Industrial Lowestoft, 1560-1730* (University of East Anglia, Ph.D., September 1991).

Colman, T., *An Historical and Topographical Handbook of Lowestoft* (Lowestoft, 1858).

Cook, G. S., *Guide to Lowestoft* (Lowestoft, c.1888).

Craik, S., *Lowestoft through the Ages* (Lowestoft, Weathercock Press, 1979).

Gillingwater, E., *Historical Account of the ancient town of Lowestoft* (1790).

Godden, G. A., *The Illustrated Guide to Lowestoft Porcelain* (London, Herbert Jenkins, 1969).

Jenkins, F., *Port War: Lowestoft 1939-45* (Ipswich, W. H. Cowell, 1946).

Lees, H. D. W., *The Chronicles of a Suffolk Parish Church* (Lowestoft, published by the author, 1949).

Longe, F. D., *Lowestoft in Olden Times* (Lowestoft, 1898, 1905).

The Lowestoft Guide, containing a descriptive account of Lowestoft and its environs, by a Lady (Yarmouth, 1812).

Malster, R. W., *Lowestoft, east coast port* (Lavenham, Terence Dalton, 1982).

Mitchley, J., *The Story of the Lowestoft Lifeboats, 1801-1876* (Lowestoft Libraries, 1974).

Moore, R. W., *On Service: The Story of the Lowestoft Lifeboats* (Lowestoft, 1977).

Powell, M. L., *Lowestoft through the Ages* (Lowestoft, Flood & Son, 1951).

Rose, J. E., *Jack Rose's Lowestoft* (Lowestoft, Panda, 1981).

Rose, J. E., *Jack Rose's Lowestoft Album* (Lowestoft, Panda, 1983).

Rose, J. E., *Jack Rose's Lowestoft Scrapbook* (Lowestoft, Panda, 1988).

Rose, J. E., *Lowestoft Then and Now* (Lowestoft Archaeological and Local History Society, 1973 and later editions).

Stather Hunt, B. P. W., *Pakefield: The Church and Village* (Pakefield, 1938).

Steward, A. V., *Lowestoft, town against the sea* (Norwich, Jarrold & Sons, 1950).

Turner, N., *Lowestoft China Bicentenary: exhibition catalogue* (Ipswich Corporation Museums Committee, 1957).

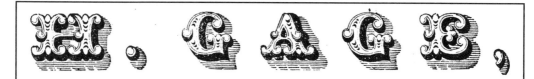

H. GAGE,

LICENSED TO LET

HORSES FOR HIRE,

CROWN HOTEL YARD,

LOWESTOFT.

BROUGHAMS, OPEN CARRIAGES,

Basket Phætons, Gigs, & Dog Carts.

Wedding Carriages, Hearse & Mourning Coaches

AT THE SHORTEST NOTICE.

*** OMNIBUS AND CABS TO MEET ALL TRAINS.